Resolving Apparent Contradictions in the Bible

Advenigo C Casido

ISBN: 978-1-78364-509-1

www.obt.org.uk

Unless indicated otherwise Scripture quotations are from The Authorized (King James) Version. Rights in the Authorized Version in the United Kingdom are vested in the Crown. Reproduced by permission of the Crown's patentee, Cambridge University Press.

****

The Open Bible Trust
Fordland Mount, Upper Basildon
Reading, RG8 8LU, UK.

Resolving Apparent Contradictions in the Bible

Contents

Page

5	Foreword
9	Introduction
13	Apparent Contradictions?
21	1. Problems in Understanding
21	Reading into the Text
22	Inaccurate Reading
23	Incomplete Reading
30	Proving/Testing Things that Differ
33	2. Translation Problems
43	3. Transmission Problems
51	In Summary
54	About the Author
55	More on this Subject
61	About this Book

Foreword

Foreword

It is easy, in this current day and age, to be tempted into thinking that, perhaps, the Bible isn't the infallible Word of an infallible God. Influences abound which would have us believe that a set of documents thousands of years old, as the Scriptures are, could not possibly stand up to examination in today's age of enlightened thinking and research methods. The author does not agree - he maintains that the Biblical record holds up to scrutiny, and can indeed be relied upon.

Mr Casido identifies three distinct problem areas which have led some to question the reliability and consistency of the Bible. This booklet is an attempt to address such problem areas, to work through the issues involved, and to restore the reader's confidence in the Bible and the words which God has preserved for us.

David Tavender
President of the Berean Bible Fellowship of Australia

Introduction

Introduction

Some suppose that our Bible is not inspired by God and so cannot be relied upon because of the inconsistencies they think it contains. They can easily cite some discrepancies between two or more passages of Scripture. Other Christians, who do believe the Bible to be the inspired word of God, think that these accusers have an axe to grind, and consider their scepticism as sacrilege, and so dismiss the apparent inconsistency without due process and further scrutiny.

Apparent Contradictions?

Apparent Contradictions?

Those who maintain that there are contradictions among the biblical passages can tabulate many of them. For instance: compare 2 Samuel 24:13 with 1 Chronicles 21:11-12:

> 2 Samuel 24:13: So Gad came to David, and told him, and said unto him, Shall *seven* years of famine come unto thee in thy land? or wilt thou flee three months before thine enemies, while they pursue thee? or that there be three days' pestilence in thy land? now advise, and see what answer I shall return to him that sent me.

> 1 Chronicles 21:11-12: So Gad came to David, and said unto him, Thus saith the Lord, Choose thee either *three* years' famine; or three months to be destroyed before thy foes, while that the sword of thine enemies overtaketh thee; or else three days the sword of the Lord, even the pestilence, in the land, and the angel of the Lord destroying throughout all the coasts of Israel. Now therefore advise thyself what word I shall bring again to him that sent me.

According to 2 Samuel, one of the options Jehovah gave David through Gad was "*seven* years of famine come unto thee in thy land" (7 years). However, according to 1 Chronicles, one of the options was "*three* years' famine" (3 years). Here there is a difference of four years that essentially presents a contradiction, but is this the original or has a copying error been made by some human scribe?

Resolving Apparent Contradictions in the Bible

Again, compare 2 Chronicles 36:9 with 2 Kings 24:8:

> 2 Chronicles 36:9: Jehoiachin was *eight* years old when he began to reign, and he reigned three months and ten days in Jerusalem: and he did that which was evil in the sight of the Lord.

> 2 Kings 24:8: Jehoiachin was *eighteen* years old when he began to reign, and he reigned in Jerusalem three months. And his mother's name was Nehushta, the daughter of Elnathan of Jerusalem.

The chronicler recorded that "Jehoiachin was *eight* years old when he began to reign, and he reigned three months and ten days in Jerusalem." While in the 2 Kings record "Jehoiachin was *eighteen* years old when he began to reign, and he reigned in Jerusalem three months." Of course, eight and eighteen is no tolerable difference, but was that difference in the original scriptures or has there been another human transmission error some years later when copying another manuscript?

Compare 1 Kings 4:26 with 2 Chronicles 9:25. The former records: "And Solomon had *forty* thousand stalls of horses for his chariots, and twelve thousand horsemen." The latter accounts: "And Solomon had *four* thousand stalls for horses and chariots, and twelve thousand horsemen." Again, such an error is easy for a human copyist to make. We may not know which is the correct number, but this does not upset the faith of one who believes the original manuscripts were inspired by God.

Another type of apparent discrepancy is found in Matthew 21:7 with Mark 11:7:

Resolving Apparent Contradictions in the Bible

Matthew 21:6-7: And the disciples went, and did as Jesus commanded them, and brought the ass, and the colt, and put on them their clothes, and they set him thereon.

Mark 11:7: And they brought the colt to Jesus, and cast their garments on him; and he sat upon him.

Matthew wrote that Christ's two disciples "brought the ass, and the colt, and put on them their clothes, and they sat him thereon," while Mark accounted that the two disciples "brought the colt to Jesus, and cast their garments on him; and he sat upon him." Undoubtedly, these two accounts have an apparent discrepancy for the former records two (the ass and the colt), while the latter records only the colt. However, there need be no contradiction here. John 12:15 states that Jesus rode on the colt, and as that was the animal Jesus rode on, Mark saw that animal as significant (as it fulfilled Old Testament prophecy, Zechariah 9:9) and so may not have felt it necessary to mention the ass.

If we compare Matthew 26:7 with John 12:3 we have another contradiction, according to some people. Matthew's account traces that a certain woman came unto Jesus with a "precious ointment, and poured it on His head, as he sat at meat." In the other passage, John identified the woman as Mary and proclaimed that she "anointed the feet of Jesus, and wiped His feet with her hair." The argument is clear; the head of Jesus is not His feet, but a reading of the context shows that these were two separate occasions. The first took place in the home of Simon the Leper (Matthew 26:7), while the second took place at the home of Mary, Martha and Lazarus (John 12:1-3). Here, clearly, there is no contradiction.

These, and many other *apparent* contradictions that are scattered in the pages of our Bible, are cited, without effort to resolve them, by some who criticize the Christian faith and by doing so have destroyed the confidence of some Christians in the authority of the Bible.

But what do we really believe concerning this matter? We believe that the *original writings* were the inerrant **Word of God**, that they did not contain any errors or contradictions, either of details in passages or doctrines. Any contradictions of details or doctrines that occur in the manuscripts now in our possession are but human interpolations or misunderstandings.

Moreover, we believe that the copies of the manuscripts of the Bible that we do have today are so accurate and reliable, that we should base all our doctrines and practices on the Bible. It should be the final authority, for the errors we find within these copies, caused by human hand, are minor. Therefore, we feel that it is our fundamental duty to defend the veracity of the Bible and to attempt to resolve any seeming contradictions. In our endeavour to resolve the difficult passages or apparent contradictions in the Bible, we have come up with three distinct, but equally important, aspects by which errors have crept into some parts of Christianity, namely understanding, translation, and transmission.

1.
Problems in Understanding

1. Problems in Understanding

Firstly, we identify doctrinal errors under the heading of understanding. It is our humble confession that we found errors in some Christian doctrines which are actually due to misunderstanding certain passages in the Bible. We call errors under this heading "Understanding Errors" and this refers to the traditional thoughts, doctrines or interpretations that cannot actually be supported by the biblical passages claimed to support them. Some are due to wrong interpretation; others are due to the error of treating similar accounts in different books of the Bible as identical. Others still are dispensational problems. Some result from ignorance of the science of correct interpretation, and others from the preference of tradition over the Bible.

(a) Reading into the Text

Some read into the Bible what is actually not there. I call this "importation of traditional teachings." For example, tradition teaches that Adam and Eve ate an apple in the Garden of Eden. However, if we examine the biblical records, we cannot find an apple mentioned, but a "fruit" of the tree of the knowledge of good and evil (Genesis 2:17; 3:6). We are not actually told what fruit it is; it is not named. But tradition imported an "apple" into the passage, thus committing an error.

Another example is the common belief that the infant Jesus was visited by three Kings from the East. Here is a demonstration of a tradition being believed by the popular society which is actually unscriptural. First, we point out that the Bible does not say these were kings who visited Jesus, but Magi or Wise Men (Matthew 2:1). This is an illustration of reading into the passage what is not there.

Also, some traditions have gone further by assigning names to the supposed three kings - Baltazzar, Gaspar, and Melchur. And many of its proponents just blindly follow in full agreement of this unverified interpolation. As to how many Magi had visited the infant Jesus, we are not actually told. There are an unspecified number of the wise men. We are only certain that there were more than one. There could have been two, three, four or more. The idea that there were three originates from the fact that they brought three gifts, but we are told only the number of gifts they brought, rather than how many brought them. There could have been just two: one could have brought both gold and myrrh, and the other frankincense. However, we do not know how many Magi there were.

(b) Inaccurate Reading

It is commonly believed and taught that Elijah was carried into the heavens on a chariot of fire pulled by horses of fire. But that's pure and simple tradition! The Bible's teaching is found in 2 Kings 2:9-11 (compare with 2:1). Verse 11 says, "And it came to pass, as they still went on, and talked, that, behold, there appeared a chariot of fire, and horses of fire, and parted them both asunder; and Elijah went up by a whirlwind into heaven." Now then, what carried Elijah into the heavens? It was a whirlwind.

(c) Incomplete Reading

Noah and the animals

A text is a part of a larger context. And it is foolish not to take notice of the whole story, picture or idea, in which a text is found. For instance, how many sheep got into Noah's Ark? A majority of respondents answer "Two - a male and a female." When asked where they learned it from, they cite the Scripture as their source. But, when we open the Bible, we are told that God's command was "of every clean beast thou shalt take to thee by *sevens*, the male and his female" and of "beasts that are not clean by *two*, the male and his female" (Genesis 7:2). Sheep are declared to be clean beasts, thus there were seven. But where did the tradition of there being only two originate? Of course it is based on a biblical passage, Genesis 6:19; "And of every living thing of all flesh, two of every sort shalt thou bring into the ark, to keep them alive with thee; they shall be male and female."

It seems, to some, that there is a contradiction between these two passages. But we maintain that God's Word never contradicts itself, that the problem involved here is one of failure to understand the passage accurately. Genesis 6:19 does not contain any error. Correct reading will lead us to right understanding. The key is "they shall be male and female." It is correct that the command of "two of every sort" is the "male and his female" or in simple language, "by pairs." But of *how many* pairs, we are told in the next chapter. Genesis 7:2-3 provides the answer of how many pairs. "Of every clean beast ... by sevens ... and of beasts that are not clean by two ...." Remove the traditional belief, let the Scripture explain itself, and the contradiction vanishes.

Noah in the ark

Another example of this failure is in the case of how long Noah and his family stayed in the ark. For some reason or other, some tell us that it was 40 days and 40 nights. Others offer a variety of answers, but with no certainty. This situation is the result of taking a part of the picture, story or idea as the whole. This difficulty can be erased when we take all the pieces of the question, "How long did Noah and his family stay in the ark?"

Let's take Genesis 7:11-13:

> In the sixth hundredth year of Noah's life, in the second month, the seventeenth day of the month, the same day were all the fountains of the great deep broken up, and the windows of heaven were opened ... In the self same day entered Noah, and Shem, and Ham ...

This provides us with the first part of the whole story; 600th year, 2nd month, on the 17th day, Noah and his family entered into the ark. The next point to complete the equation is the date of Noah's life when they got out from the ark. Genesis 8:13-18 provides it:

> And it came to pass in the six hundredth and first year, in the first month, the first day of the month, the waters were dried up from off the earth: and Noah removed the covering of the ark, and looked, and, behold, the face of the ground was dry. And in the second month, on the seven and twentieth day of the month, was the earth dried. And God spoke unto Noah, saying "Go forth of the ark, thou, and thy wife, and thy sons and thy sons' wives with thee. And Noah went forth."

This gives us the exact date when they got out from the ark, i.e., 601st year, 2nd month on the 27th day. Now let's join the pieces together to get the whole picture:

Year	Month	Day
601	2	27 - Noah and his family went forth
600	2	17 - Noah and his family entered
1	0	10 - Days in the ark

The total days of Noah and his family in the ark: 1 year and 10 days. There is accuracy!

Enoch not found

Did Enoch die?

> By faith Enoch was translated that he should not see death; and was not found. (Hebrews 11:5)

It is a common belief that Enoch did not die. However, I humbly disagree with this view, with due respect to God's power to do things we cannot explain. But what of certain passages such as Hebrews 11:5, which seem to clearly teach that he did not die? I feel a responsibility to re-examine this common view due to some apparent contradictions and inconsistencies Hebrews 11:5 has with other passages and doctrines in the Bible.

The first difficulty that struck me is the later statement by the writer of the Hebrews in verse 13 of the same chapter. This declares:

> These all died in faith ...

And this would include Enoch!

The next difficulty was the startling inconsistency between the common belief that Enoch did not die with that of another statement in Hebrews.

> And as it is appointed unto men once to die, but after this the judgment. (Hebrews 9:27)

Again, this would include Enoch and this is reinforced by Romans 5:12:

> Wherefore, as by one man sin entered into the world, and death by sin; and so death passed upon all men, for that all have sinned.

"All men" would include Enoch. However, to those who object that the latter passage refers only to the spiritual death of Adam, and that Adam and Eve did not experience immediate physical death after committing the sin, we may answer them with a threefold question: If their supposition is true, then what is the cause of physical death, when did it start, and why?

To those who want to play on exceptions to "all die", claiming there will be those who will not experience physical death at the coming of the Lord Jesus Christ, we appeal to their common sense. The return of the Lord is a future, exceptional event and we will not deny that those who will remain and are alive at the coming of the Lord will not taste death (1 Thessalonians 4:16-17).

Nonetheless, it is always our rule in biblical hermeneutics that we will only endorse an exception where the Bible endorses that exception. In this case therefore, we cannot include Enoch among those who will not die because Enoch lived and died long before the exception will take place; that is, at the coming of our Lord.

Furthermore, if Enoch was changed from a mortal body to an immortal one (for neither blood nor flesh can enter into the kingdom of God), then he can no longer be touched by death. And if, as some suppose, Enoch will be one of the witnesses in Revelation chapter 11, then he is still in his mortal body for the two witnesses will be killed by the beast that ascends out of the bottomless pit (Revelation 11:7).

It would seem then that the meaning of Hebrews 11:5, and Genesis 5:24, is that Enoch was translated so that he would not taste death at that time. But the teaching of the rest of Scripture was that he would die later. When Philip was caught away by the Spirit, he was translated to a different part of the land, (Acts 8:39-40). Could this be the sort of thing that happened to Enoch?

Where is Enoch Now?

However, if Enoch is alive unto this day then where is he now? Many suppose that he is enjoying sweet fellowship with God in heaven or in Paradise. This, too, is questionable. It nullifies the hope of resurrection for it supposes that there is life and fellowship in heaven with man and God without resurrection.

Moreover, if we will insist on believing that Enoch is now in heaven, then Enoch had to have ascended to heaven, for how could he be in heaven without ascending there first? Believing this assumption, however, will contradict the clear statement of John 3:13:

> No man hath ascended up to heaven, but he that came down from heaven, even the Son of man.

Of no doubt, David was a righteous and great man of God, but it is a clear testimony of Scripture that "David is not ascended into the heavens" (Acts 2:34).

It is then my humble conclusion that out of consistent examination of the basic teaching in the Scripture, Enoch did not taste death at some point in his life when there was a particular danger (as the testimony of Hebrews 11:5) but later on he died, as the testimony of Hebrews 11:13, and the general teachings of the Bible, make it clear.

But on what does tradition base its belief that Enoch did not die? It is derived from Hebrews 11:5: "By faith Enoch was translated that he should not see death." We may then ask a question: What does "translated" mean?

The word "translated" is a translation of the Greek word *metatitheme*. According to Dr. E.W. Bullinger in his *Critical Lexicon and Concordance to the N.T., metatitheme* means to put or place in another place, to transport. And Dr. Strong in his *Exhaustive Concordance* gives the same basic idea: "*metatitheme* literally means transport." *A Greek-English Lexicon of the New Testament and Other Early Christian Literature* by Bauer, translated by Arndt and Gingrich testifies the same: convey to another place, put in other place, transfer. Dr. E. Vine in his *Expository Dictionary* gives the same testimony: to transfer to another place. Moreover, the same Greek word *metatitheme* is used in Acts 7:16 and is rightly translated "carried over."

So then, we refer back to our previous declaration that Enoch was translated, transported, carried over from one place to another that he should not see death at that particular danger, but, as the general teaching of the Scripture, he must have died later in his life, which totalled 365 years.

Now let's examine another important evidence of Enoch's death. "And all the days of Enoch were three hundred sixty and five years" (Genesis 5:23). If he is alive yet; if he never died, 365 years falls very far short of expressing the 4,000+ years, so far, of Enoch's life! "All the days of Enoch" is a phrase which indicates a limitation of days. Three hundred and sixty five years states "all the days" Enoch *lived*. The implication of the very expression is that he did, at some point, die.

One more thing is the examination of the phrase "and he was not" (Genesis 5:24). "And he died" was said of all who were named from Adam onwards ... Enoch excepted. For him rather a different phrase was used: "and he was not." But what does this phrase really mean? Some people understand it to mean he was no longer on earth; that he was translated to heaven. This view our Lord flatly denies (John 3:13), as we have mentioned. However, in Lamentations 5:7 we have this statement: "Our fathers have sinned, and are not." Whatever happened to Enoch when he "was not", happened also to the fathers when they "are not". Therefore, if the words, "and he was not" mean that Enoch was immortalized, so were the fathers; if he was translated to the heavens, so were they! But that was not the case, "our fathers have sinned, and are not," must mean our fathers sinned and have died. Indeed, it is affirmed that they did not live forever, but that they died (Zechariah. 1:5; John 8:52; Hebrews 11:13).

Accordingly, the occurrence of this statement in the book of Genesis clearly endorses our findings; for it must be admitted that a writer has the right to interpret his own writing. Every time Moses used this expression, he meant death. In Genesis 42:36,

Jacob in great sorrow thinking that Joseph was dead he said "Me ye have bereaved of my children; Joseph *is not*, and Simeon *is not*, and ye will take Benjamin away." That Jacob means Joseph was dead is positively stated in Genesis 42:38: "My son shall not go down with you; for his brother *is dead*." Reuben, like his father, expressed it in Genesis 37:30: "the child is not".

It is therefore my contention that the Bible cannot and will not contradict itself on such an important subject as this. Thus, as it is said "death passed upon all men", and "as it is appointed unto men once to die" it means what it says. And when it, after naming the heroes of faith, including Enoch, states "all these died," and in other passages it declares "all the days of Enoch was 365 years" and that he "was not" we humbly submit to the Bible and conclude that Enoch died. And when it says that "no man hath ascended up to the heaven," our view that Enoch was not translated into heaven is endorsed.

(d) Proving/Testing the Things that Differ

Some problems, or apparent contradictions, are caused by the failure to distinguish the things that differ, confusing what is said to Jews with what is said to Gentiles, or comparing a statement made in one dispensation with that which belongs to another dispensation. Failure to separate truth applicable only to one dispensation from other truths that are exclusive to other dispensations is a fruitful cause of misconception, confusion and apparent contradiction. Not knowing the dispensational thrust of the Bible closes the door to right interpretation and can result in misunderstandings. Let's look at some examples.

Circumcision
- You must be circumcised. If you are not circumcised, you are cut off from God's people; (see Genesis 17:9-14).
- Gentiles must not practice circumcision. If they practice circumcision, Christ will be of no profit to them; (see Galatians 5.2).

An Unbelieving Mate
- If your wife is an unbeliever, you must separate from her (see Ezra 10:2-12).
- If your wife is an unbeliever, do not separate from her; (see 1 Corinthians 7:12-14; and note 1 Peter 3:1-6).

Eating Pork
- Pork is unclean and must not be eaten (see Leviticus 11:7-8).
- Pork is not necessarily unclean and may be eaten (see 1 Timothy. 4:3-5).

The Sabbath
- The Sabbath must be observed (see Exodus. 20:8).
- The Sabbath need not be observed (see Galatians 4:9-11; Colossians 2:16).

Ordinances
- Ordinances must be obeyed (see Leviticus 18:1-4; Numbers 9:14).
- Ordinances have been abolished (see Ephesians 2:15; Colossians 2:14).

Resolving Apparent Contradictions in the Bible

Every passage in the Bible has a dispensational context that needs to be considered if we wish to understand it correctly, and if we wish to make valid applications to our dispensation of grace. In the above apparent contradictions, the first statement applies to Jews under the Law of Moses, whereas the second applies generally to Gentiles under grace.

There are many doctrines in the Bible that traverse dispensations (for example, God is love, a fact that is true to every dispensation). However, there are teachings exclusive to a specific dispensation which, when imported to other dispensations, will create contradictions, as we have just seen. If you come across an apparent contradiction, then check each statement to see who it is said to or about, a Jew or a Gentile, and check to see in which dispensation each statement is made. If you do this and the difficulty persists, then the problem may be caused by translation.

2. Translation Problems

2. Translation Problems

Translation problems are caused by the difficulty of translating the original languages used in the Bible into English, and other languages or dialects, like Cebuano. Errors have crept into translation for several reasons.

Most, if not all, theologians agree that the so-called "Old Testament" books were originally written in Hebrew and partly Aramaic, while the New Testament books were written originally in Greek (*Koine* Greek). The most popularly known *Authorized Version*, or the *King James Version* of 1611, is actually a direct translation of the manuscript known as the *Textus Receptus* or the Received Text.

In the process of translation from the original languages to that of English and/or other dialects, errors have crept into the text in a few instances. The vast majority of these are somewhat unintentional, but equally unfortunate. Sometimes, however, translators commit an error of translation to let the text fit their private theology. Sometimes tradition blinded the translators. Some errors are the product of the problem of translating the richer language (Greek) to a less rich language (English).

Punctuation

In a few cases, punctuation is misplaced, which, in effect, alters the real sense of the passage. The original languages used in the writing of the books in the Bible, in their primitive structure, have no punctuation marks. For example, let us examine Luke 23:43, "And Jesus said unto him, Verily I say unto thee, Today shalt thou be with me in Paradise." From this declaration of Jesus Christ, it appears on the surface that on that very day, the malefactor went with Christ to Paradise and lives there unto this day. But from other passages of the Scripture it is very clear that Paradise is to be established in the future, and that those who are asleep in Christ are still waiting for their resurrection (1 Corinthians 15:51-52; 1 Thessalonians 4:13-16). This then creates a difficulty, an apparent contradiction. Furthermore, the Lord Jesus Christ did not go to Paradise at that day but went to *Hades* and stayed in the heart of the earth three days and three nights. Where was the malefactor then?

However, the real sense of the passage is discovered by just relocating the misplaced comma to its proper place. Thus, Luke 23:43 should read, "And Jesus said unto him, `Verily I say unto thee today [comma], thou shalt be with me in Paradise.'" This is not an attempt to alter Scripture to fit to our theology, but it ensures this verse fits in with the rest of the Bible. It also recognises that the phrase "I say unto thee today" is a Hebraism, or a Hebrew idiom, used to give emphasis, as can be seen from its use in such places as Deuteronomy 4:26,39,40; 5:1; 6:6; 7:11; Joshua 23:14, etc.

Thou Shalt Not Kill

Let us consider a translation error. Exodus 20:13 states, "Thou shalt not kill", but if we take this at face value we do not get very far before we meet a difficulty, an apparent contradiction. The very next chapter, Exodus 21, gives commandments to kill people. Consider the following verses.

Verse 12: He that smiteth a man, so that he die, shall be surely put to death.

Verse 15: And he that smiteth his father, or his mother, shall be surely put to death.

Verse 16: And he that stealeth a man, and selleth him, or if he be found in his hand, he shall surely be put to death.

"Shall be put to death" is a contradiction of "Thou shalt not kill." With the help of a Hebrew Interlinear, we discover that the Hebrew word translated "kill" in Exodus 20:13 is *ratsach*. According to the *Hebrew-English Lexicon of the Old Testament* by Brown, Driver and Briggs, *ratsach* means 'to murder, slay' from an Aramaic word which means 'to break, bruise - murder, slay with premeditation.' Dr. James Strong in the Hebrew Dictionary found in his *Exhaustive Concordance*, defines the word *ratsach* as "to dash in pieces, i.e., kill (a human being), especially to murder." The word is translated "murder" by the translators of the New International Version, and many other modern translations. What is basically the difference between "kill" and "murder?" Upon consulting the Merriam-Webster Dictionary we find a very substantial difference between them, which is essential to our discovery. 'Kill' is a mere deprivation of life while 'murder' is a crime of unlawfully killing a person, especially with malice aforethought.

We then come to a conclusion that the correct translation of the Hebrew word *ratsach* is "murder", as favoured by the most modern translations. Hence, "thou shalt not murder" (Exodus 20:13) is the correct rendering, and this eradicates the apparent contradiction between this verse and "put to death" (Exodus 21:12,15,16), which are provisions for the lawful taking of an offender's life.

Saul

If we turn to 1 Samuel 28:6 we read, "And when Saul enquired of the Lord, the Lord answered him not ..." We know from this verse that Saul enquired of the Lord. But turning to the account of 1 Chronicles 10 we see a different declaration. It says in verses 13 and 14, "So Saul died for his transgression which he committed against the Lord, even against the word of the Lord, which he kept not, and also for asking counsel of one that had a familiar spirit, to enquire of it; and enquired not of the Lord ..." From this record we are certain that Saul "enquired *not* of the Lord," which seems to contradict the previous text which tells us that Saul "enquired of the Lord."

This is another error of translation, for upon looking into a Hebrew Interlinear we discover that the original word translated "enquire" in these texts are not the same, but two different words. The Hebrew word used in 1 Samuel 28:6 is *sha'al* which is translated "enquire." In 1 Chronicles 10:14 the Hebrew word used is *darash*, which is also translated "enquire."

Dr. E. W. Bullinger in *The Companion Bible* noted this discrepancy. In his note on 1 Chronicles 10:14, he wrote:

> "to enquire - to seek and consult. Hebrew *darash*, to seek earnestly. Saul sought thus with the medium, but not with Jehovah."

Accordingly, his note on 1 Samuel 28:6 is:

> "enquired - asked. Heb. *sha'al*, to ask. Not *darash*, 'to seek out.'"

In the Hebrew Dictionary of *Strong's Exhaustive Concordance*, Dr. James Strong appears to give distinction between these two words, *darash* being intensive as to enquire diligently or make an inquisition, while *sha'al* has an idea of merely asking but not seeking out the matter. The *Hebrew-English Lexicon of the Old Testament* by Brown, Driver & Briggs affirms our point that *sha'al* means "ask, enquire, petition" while *darash* means;

> "to resort to, to seek out; an equivalent to an Aramaic word which means rub over, discuss, search out."

With this information, therefore, we conclude that Saul did *sha'al* (enquire) to the Lord but he did not *darash* (seek earnestly) to the Lord. When we notice that there are two different words in the Hebrew, then the contradiction vanishes.

Age / World

Hebrews 1:1-2 states:

> God, who at sundry times and in divers manners spake in time past unto the fathers by the prophets, hath in these last days spoken unto us by his Son, whom he hath appointed heir of all things, by whom also he made the worlds.

The Greek word translated 'worlds' is *aionas*, a plural form of *aion*. The *KJV* translates the word *aion* into English with the word "world" in many or most instances. However, the *NIV* in some places changed it to the English word "age," which is a better translation. For instance, see Matthew 12:32; 13:39,40,49, and many more.

However, the *NIV* has committed a translation error with *aion* in Hebrews 1:2, wherein it translates it "universe," which is an inconsistent and poor rendering. We do not see any valid reason for it doing so, and conclude that it must come only from a personal preference of the translators.

Dr. E.W. Bullinger has a note on the word *aion* in his *Critical Lexicon*:

> "*aion* ... the space of a human life, an age or generation in respect of duration ... The time lived or to be lived by men, time as moving, historical time as well as eternity ..."

Same Word - Different Translation
Another problem caused by translation involves altering the translation of a particular word from one place to another when there's no warrant to do so. For example:

> Hebrews 7:22: By so much was Jesus made a surety of a better *testament*.
> Hebrews 8:6: But now hath he obtained a more excellent ministry, by how much also he is the mediator of a better *covenant*, which was established upon better promises.

The Greek word *diatheke* is found in both passages. The former translates *diatheke* into "testament" while the latter translates it by "covenant". This error has been put right by the translators of the *NIV*.

Conversely sometimes, a problem of translating two different Hebrew or Greek words into one English word occurs. For instance, the aforementioned problem of translating the word *darash* and *sha'al* into one English word "enquire." Another example is the word "hell" in the New Testament, which is actually used to translate two different Greek words: *hades* and *gehenna*. If the common belief that hell is the lake of fire is true, then a problem is introduced, because in Revelation 20:14 *hades* (hell) is thrown into the lake of fire (hell). Hell seems to be thrown into itself!!! References for hell (*hades*) come in Mathew 11:23; 16:18; Luke 10:15, etc. and references for hell (*gehenna*) are in Matthew 5:22,29; 10:28; 18:9, etc.

So then, when we face apparent contradictions in passages, translation is one factor to be considered and by comparing different translations of the Bible, or even different manuscripts, the contradiction may be resolved.

3. Transmission Problems

3. Transmission Problems

Transmission problems refer to the errors that occur in the process of copying a text; that is, when scribes copied from Hebrew to Hebrew or from Greek to Greek, and we have already mentioned some of these earlier on pages 4 and 5. With the absence of the printing press, handwriting was used to make another copy of a text in the same language. By copying they intended to preserve the original text so that they could hand down a text that would be the same as the original. Charles Welch has a good comment on this when he writes:

> "Before the invention of printing, every book, of necessity, was written by hand. This manuscript work, however faithfully undertaken, becomes, in time, partly automatic, and slight errors are bound to occur. When we remember that, in some cases, the scribe was a poor, badly educated believer, making his copy in secret, under the shadow of possible apprehension and martyrdom, we can understand how the possibilities of error to transcription were multiplied. (*The Volume of the Book*, Berean Publishing Trust, pp. 37-38).

Yet, if the reader will stop and think for the moment, none of these errors need prevent him from finding out what the original text was. Suppose this booklet was given to twenty different people to copy, people of all grades of education and appreciation of the subject matter. It is possible that one copy would be absolutely free from any errors, but which one? A careful examination of all twenty would enable any judicious reader to discover the original text, for it's certain that where, say, five would make the same mistake, the other fifteen would correct it.

Today, we do not have the original manuscripts written by the first writers and upon which our Bibles are based. Nevertheless, there are many Hebrew and Greek manuscripts available which are used to translate the Bible into English. These various manuscripts differ in some respects, and that is reflected in different versions, but none of these versions differ significantly as copying (transmission) errors tend to be of a minor nature.

These various manuscripts were products of the believers who made copies of the text. In the process however, two probable types of transmission errors could have, and did, occur.

Transmission errors might be by omission or insertion (addition)

To demonstrate our point we will use the *New International Version* (*NIV*) as our model. But before giving some illustration, I will quote part of the preface of the *NIV* concerning the manuscript used by the translators.

> For the Old Testament, The Standard Hebrew Text, the Masoretic Text as published in the latest editions of *Biblia Hebraica*, was used throughout. The Dead Sea Scrolls contain material bearing on an earlier stage of the Hebrew text. They were consulted, as were the Samaritan Pentateuch and the ancient scribal traditions relating to textual changes. Sometimes a variant Hebrew reading in the margin of the Masoretic Text was followed instead of the text itself. Such instances, being variants within the Masoretic tradition, are not specified by footnotes. In rare

Resolving Apparent Contradictions in the Bible

cases, words in the consonantal text were divided differently from the way they appear in the Masoretic Text. Footnotes indicate this. The translators also consulted the more important early versions - the Septuagint; Aquila, Symmachus and Theodotion; the Vulgate; the Syriac Peshitta; the Targums; and for the Psalms the Juxta *Hebraica* of Jerome. Readings from these versions were occasionally followed where the Masoretic Text seemed doubtful and where accepted principles of Textual Criticism showed that one or more of these textual witnesses appeared to provide correct reading. Such instances are footnoted. Sometimes, vowel signs did not, in the judgment of the translators, present the correct vowels for the original consonant text. Accordingly some words were read with a different set of vowels. These instances are usually not indicated by footnotes.

The Greek text used in translating the New Testament was an eclectic one. No other piece of ancient literature has such an abundance of manuscript witnesses as does the New Testament. Where existing manuscripts differ, the translators made their choice of readings according to accepted principles of the New Testament textual criticism. Footnotes call attention to places where there was uncertainty about what the original text was. The best current printed texts of the Greek New Testament were used.

Obviously, the *NIV* translators consulted more than one manuscript and were confronted with alternative renderings. They recognized the problem of transmission errors and followed the principles of New Testament textual criticism, the process used to recover the original text.

Earlier, I noted two major types of transmission errors, viz., an omission and an insertion. "Often it is the result of two lines of the manuscript ending with the same word. The eye of the copyist falls upon the second line instead of the first so that the whole line is omitted; or the process may be reversed, and the whole line repeated" (from *The Volume of the Book* by Charles Welch).

Transmission errors can be mechanical, mental or intentional. Mechanical, like the aforementioned, are easily corrected by comparison with other manuscripts. Mental and intentional alterations can be very serious and may be more difficult to deal with.

Mental alterations occur when something goes on in the copyist's mind, and in a momentary lapse of concentration, a wrong word is inserted. A very common form of this error is the alteration of the passage to one that is remembered in another part of the book. For example, the words of Luke 6:48 in the *KJV* are identical with those of the parallel passage in Matthew 7:25, "For it was founded upon a rock." However, some Greek manuscripts have different words in Luke 6:48 and some authorities suppose that the Revisers were correct in preferring these and rendering it as "because it had been well builded"; see also the *NIV*. It is supposed that the manuscript that had the same words in Luke and Matthew was copied by a scribe whose mind retained the Matthew reading, although his eye read what the *RV* has in the text. (See *The Volume of the Book* by Charles Welch.)

Sometimes in the process of copying, parts were left out, were later noticed and added in the upper space or in the margin; but later on another copyist omitted that section, thinking that it was not actually part of the original text. Conversely, sometimes, some put their personal opinion as a note in the margin, which was then copied by the copyist thinking that it was part of the original text. However, by comparing different manuscripts, it is easy to see these mistakes.

Hebrew and Greek manuscripts are scattered all over the world in libraries, private collections and museums - these have all or nearly all, been examined. The fact that copies of the scriptures were multiplied all over the earth, and were connected with differing schools of thought, provided an effective check in nearly all cases.

For illustration, look at 1 John 3:1: "and that is what we are" is absent from the *KJV*, but is recovered in the *NIV*. On the other hand, 1 John 5:7 in most manuscripts simple says: "for there are three that testify". The *KJV* rendering has more words, adding, "in heaven, the Father, the Word, and the Holy Ghost: and these three are one." This shows that the manuscript from which it was translated had had these extra words inserted.

Additional examples are John 3:13 - "which is in heaven" is added. John 5:4 - the whole verse was added. Mark 7:16; 9:44, and others, are not found in the *NIV* and some other versions.

In Summary

In Summary

Here, then, are at least three areas which we need to be aware of, and address, in our reading and interpretation of the Bible.

1. "Understanding" Problems - apparent contradictions due to our lack of understanding of the background of the text or our misunderstanding of the text.
- a) Take care not to read into the text that which is not there.
- b) Take care to read the text accurately.
- c) Be sure to read all that is said.
- d) Observe dispensational differences.

2. Be aware of problems arising out of an inadequate translation of the text from the original language.

3. Be aware of problems arising out of missing or added words due to the transmission of the text through time.

*****

We hope we have helped you to better understand and appreciate the Word, and we urge you to keep in mind these principles when you study the Bible. And search the Scriptures, like the Bereans in Acts 17:11, who searched to see whether the things they were taught by Paul were so.

About the author

Advenigo Casido was born 1969 in Bais City, the Philippines. He was educated at Bais City High School before undergoing theological training at Metro Manila Theological Seminary and the International Grace Bible Institute of Lupagan. He then entered the ministry for a number of years before studying at Genaro Goñi Memorial College and obtaining Bachelor of Science degree in Secondary Education with a major in Mathematics, after which he then became an instructor at Negros Oriental State University for a number of years. He was married in 1998 and lives with his wife and two sons in Bayawan City in the Philippines.

Also on this subject

Introducing the Books of the Bible
Brian Sherring

There are many people today, both Christians as well as non-Christians, who are unfamiliar with the Bible. They may have their favourite passages, but what is each book about, and how do all these books and letters fit together?

That may also be the situation of many of us. We may be very familiar with John's Gospel or Ephesians, but what about Jude or Jeremiah, to say nothing of some … most …. or even all of the Minor Prophets? And where does Jude fit in with the rest of the New Testament?

The object of this well written book is to give a brief overview of what the 66 books of the Bible are about, and to place them in relationship to each other. As such it is a publication that many will find interesting and helpful to read, and have available for reference. It is also most suitable to recommend to Christian friends who may need some help in understanding the Bible.

It has three useful appendices, one containing many helpful notes.

Further details of all the book opposite, and the ones on the next pages, can be seen on

www.obt.org.uk

They can be ordered from that website and also from

The Open Bible Trust,
Fordland Mount, Upper Basildon,
Reading, RG8 8LU, UK.

They are also avaialble as eBook from Amazon and Apple and as KDP paperbacks from Amazon.

40 Problem Passages
Michael Penny

This is a sequel to Michael Penny's earlier book *Approaching the Bible* (see next page). It applies the principles set out there to *40 Problem Passages* from the Bible. In other words, it follows the advice given by Miles Coverdale. That advice was based on asking such questions as:

- "Who" were these words written to?
- "Who" were they about?
- "Where" is this to take place?
- "When" was it written?
- "When" is it about?
- "What", precisely, is said?
- "Why" did God say it, do it, or will do it?

After asking such questions, we will have a better understanding of the passage and can "apply" that passage to our lives today.

Approaching the Bible
Michael Penny

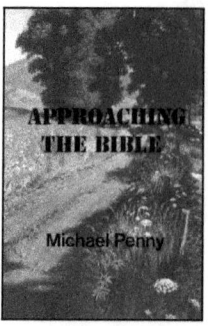

This is a thorough exposition and defence of the dispensational approach to interpreting the Bible. The author traces what he believes to be such an approach from some of the earliest Church Fathers onwards, points out the strengths and weaknesses in the dispensational system of modern interpreters, and advocates what he holds to be an improved approach.

(Reviewed by Paul C. Clark in *Librarian's World*, USA)

This is a book of sterling quality, a much needed introduction to dispensational truth, simple and lucid, but at the same time comprehensive and profound ... Dispensational truth comes across, not as a fad of certain extremists, but as a natural and inevitable result of a normal, natural and plain reading of the Bible ... A book we can without hesitation pass on or recommend to any who may inquire about our beliefs."

(Reviewed by Charles Ozanne in *Search*, GB)

A good book for those who want to study seriously the Word of God. It delves into the basic areas to lay a good foundation for understanding the message using certain guidelines set by Miles Coverdale.

(Reviewed by Frank Wren in *The Trumpet Sounds*, GB)

THE FOUNDATIONS OF DISPENSATIONAL TRUTH by E W Bullinger

This is Bullinger's last book and is his definitive work on the subject of dispensationalism. It covers the ministries of ...

- the prophets,
- the Son of God,
- those that heard Christ, and
- the ministry of Paul, the Apostle to the Gentiles.

He comments on the Gospels and the Pauline epistles and has a lengthy section on the Acts of the Apostles, followed by one explaining why miraculous signs of the Acts period ceased.

A hard-back edition is available from **www.obt.org.uk** and from

The Open Bible Trust,
Fordland Mount, Upper Basildon,
Reading, RG8 8LU, UK.

A newly typeset book, well presented in an easy to read format, is available as a KDP paperback Amazon.

It is also available as an eBook from Amazon and Kindle

About this book

Resolving Apparent Contradictions in the Bible

We are told by sceptics that the Bible contradicts itself, but is this the case? At first glance, to the uniformed or unlearned, this may *appear* to be so. However, these *apparent* contradictions are mostly resolved by considering:

1) The problems cased by translation: there is no exact 1 – 1 correspondence between the words of two different languages.
2) The problems caused by transmission: errors which arose in ancient times when manuscripts were copied by hand.
3) Problems caused by interpretation: our interpretation or understanding of the passages which *seem* to contradict is deficient.

The author does a good job in bringing before the reader these three main causes if *apparent* contradictions. He does so simply, clearly, and in a style which is easy to understand.

Publications of The Open Bible Trust must be in accordance with its evangelical, fundamental and dispensational basis. However, beyond this minimum, writers are free to express whatever beliefs they may have as their own understanding, provided that the aim in so doing is to further the object of The Open Bible Trust. A copy of the doctrinal basis is available at

www.obt.org.uk/doctrinal-basis

or from:

THE OPEN BIBLE TRUST
Fordland Mount, Upper Basildon,
Reading, RG8 8LU, GB

www.ingramcontent.com/pod-product-compliance
Lightning Source LLC
Chambersburg PA
CBHW060722030426
42337CB00017B/2962